ARIES

HOROSCOPE

& ASTROLOGY

2021

Published by Mystic Cat Press

Suite SM-2380-6403

14601 North Bybee Lake Court

Portland, Oregon 97203

Phone: +1 (805) 308-6503

islandauthor@hotmail.com

Copyright © 2020 by Mystic Cat Press

Contents

Acknowledgment:

To my family, thank you for being there and accepting my wildness.

This book is dedicated to those with an open heart, an open mind, and a willingness to plumb the mysteries of life.

You make this world a better place.

Aries 2021
Horoscope & Astrology

ARIES

Aries Dates: March 21 to April 19
Symbol: Ram
Element: Fire
Planet: Mars
House: First
Colors: Red, white

2021 inspires and delights with three gorgeous Supermoon's in the first half of the year, it is a time of fast-moving creativity and innovative thinking. They bring a message which brings a new direction. It does lead to a time where you follow a trail of potential. A gorgeous chapter beckons and brings an opportunity. It's something you dearly are hoping to achieve, this does open a door that enables you to begin developing a new goal. It does set the tone of unique and inspiring options to be revealed in 2021.

On February 12th, we ring in the Chinese New Year of the Ox, this is an important event, it brings grounded energy into your life. If you find yourself struggling with demands on your life experience in 2021, new options soon make themselves known. You are learning unique and valuable tools that help you grow. Focusing on balancing your emotions enables you to be the best you can be. You learn new techniques that will help better your ability to overcome hurdles and navigate unseen terrain with a secure foundation.

Mercury Retrograde gets up to tricks in 2021, and you discover that there may be a friendship or connection that you need to distance yourself from to be truly free from drama. An echo of the past have you noticing this aspect, you are ready to embrace developing social sties which are durable, supportive, and based on mutual respect and understanding. Although steep in the short term, you'll welcome the changes ahead, it allows you to put your best foot forward.

Solar eclipses can only occur during a New Moon phase. This is when the Moon moves between Earth and the Sun, and these three celestial bodies form a straight line: Earth–Moon–Sun.

A Lunar eclipse occurs when the earth stands between the moon and the Sun, this obscures the light of the Sun from the moon. The moon herself has no light source of her own, as she simply reflects the light of the Sun. A lunar eclipse occurs during a Full Moon and usually marks endings, transitions, or other life cycle culmination points.

Any eclipse is a significant event in astrological circles, eclipses have fascinated scientists for centuries. Eclipses are dramatic tools that instigate change in your life. An eclipse is wild, free, expansive, and explosive, the wild cards of astrology, you never quite know what you get until it happens. An eclipse can uproot, surprise, inspire, motivate, and really become an active catalyst for change. Eclipses remove the shutters, they make you aware of areas that need to be changed and often spotlight an entirely new direction to explore. Eclipses inspire change and work rapidly to see forward motion occurring.

2021 delights with three gorgeous Supermoon's. A supermoon is when the moon is at its closest approach to Earth, which occurs during a full or new moon. The effect on the ocean's tides is most significant when there is a full or new moon. This tidal force is concentrated during the super moon, it can cause the ocean tides to rise by an extra inch or two compared to a regular full moon. Super moons are they invite you to look at your life, to reveal areas which you usually keep hidden. High in the night sky, they illuminate a great deal of information should you choose to work with this sacred energy. Connecting with this information gives you a fantastic opportunity to expand your life, to reveal areas that are ready to be developed.

As the moon peaks, it naturally begins to wane, and as the moon heads towards the next gravitational peak, the new moon phase, it has a cleansing effect on your emotional awareness. This helps you remove from your life all the things that need to be released, the areas which limit progress said no real good while they are kept within your spirit. Heading into the new moon gives your excellent opportunity to connect with the mysterious darkness. It is a healing time that brings a powerful sense of cleansing. This removes the outworn energy and makes space for new opportunities to flow into your world as the moon fills once again into a full shining globe.

PLANETARY RETROGRADES

The Retrograde phase is when a planet appears, when observed from Earth, to reverse direction. This happens due to an optical illusion caused by differences in orbit. The retrograde motion can have a negative influence on your life. The planet Mercury is the best-known planet for retrograde phases. This is because Mercury is the fastest planet in our solar system, and it enters a retrograde motion between three to four times a year, for about three weeks at a time. Mercury is a planet that rules communication, so you can expect frequent misunderstandings, scheduling problems, and disagreements during a Mercury Retrograde phase. Here is a quick reference to retrogrades in 2021.

MERCURY: 3 RETROGRADES IN 2021

VENUS: 1 RETROGRADE IN 2021

MARS: NO RETROGRADE IN 2021

JUPITER: 1 RETROGRADE IN 2021

SATURN: 1 RETROGRADE IN 2021

URANUS: 2 RETROGRADE IN 2021

NEPTUNE: 1 RETROGRADE IN 2021

PLUTO: 1 RETROGRADE IN 2021

NODE: 1 RETROGRADE IN 2021

LILITH: NO RETROGRADE IN 2021

CHIRON: 1 RETROGRADE IN 2021

Aries Horoscope

Four Weeks Per Month

- Week 1 – Days 1 - 7
- Week 2 – Days 8 - 14
- Week 3 – Days 15 - 21
- Week 4 – Days 22 – Month-end

Time is set to Coordinated Universal Time Zone
(UT±0)

January 3, 4 - Quadrantids Meteor Shower.

The Quadrantids meteor shower run yearly from January 1-5. The Quadrantids meteor shower peaks this year on the night of the 3rd and morning of the 4th.

January 6 – Last Quarter Moon in Libra.

This Moon phase occurs at 09.37 UTC.

January 13 – New Moon in Capricorn.

This new moon phase occurs at 05:02 UTC. This cleans the slate and brings a fresh start. This is an excellent time to view galaxies and stars as there is no moonlight to obscure your view of the universe.

January 20 – First Quarter Moon in Aries.

This Moon phase occurs at 21.02 UTC.

January 24 – Mercury at Greatest Eastern Elongation.

The planet Mercury reaches greatest eastern elongation of 18.6 degrees from the Sun. This occurs at 02.00 UTC. Look for Mercury low in the sky just after sunset.

January 28 - Full Moon in Leo.

This full moon phase occurs at 19:16 UTC. Full Wolf Moon. This full moon has also been known as the Old Moon and the Moon After Yule.

January 29 – Jupiter in Conjunction with the Sun.

The planet Jupiter in Conjunction with the Sun. This occurs at 01:00 UTC.

January 30 – Mercury Retrograde begins in Aquarius.

During a retrograde period, it isn't the right time to move forward in any practical venture. Be prepared for misunderstandings and miscommunications to be prevalent.

JANUARY HOROSCOPE

JANUARY WEEK ONE

This is a time which links you to the past, there will be some memories, resurfacing, and it helps you resolve areas which seek to be released. A change of scene is coming, which helps you celebrate the holidays with a splash. Something new beckons, which opens a path for you to explore. Powerful options are ready to emerge in your life. It is a wonderful time of letting go and beginning to plot a course towards developing goals. You have a pleasant outlook ahead that draws change and luck into your world. You are set to benefit from an extraordinary flow of potential soon that brings new options to your door. It does see you being inspired and becoming happier in the coming months. It does put you in an excellent position to generate lucrative ideas, the path is creative, there is a strong focus on identity and self-development. You move in alignment with a vision that lights up with potential. It certainly brings happiness and good fortune to your world.

This is an outstanding time to plot a course towards new options. Planning for the year ahead will see you making incredible progress. You are likely to see your situation grow from an endeavor you pour your energy into. You revel in a lovely harmonious time in the weeks ahead, you deserve to have a break and enjoy an abundant season. An opportunity arises for you soon, which will be as sweet as sugar. It is a beautiful gift which enables you to advance your life. A new role or position is coming, and it does bring more responsibilities to your world. A dazzling array of potential is at your disposal once you receive news of this offer.

The New Moon in Capricorn reveals insight into your more profound vision. It beckons you towards a more social environment to balance the stress in your life. It is is a time that sees you running with your tribe. Breaking out with a lively atmosphere is the perfect setting from which to renew your spirit and draw abundance into your life. It does see you blending your thoughts with others who are on the same page. This could launch your big ideas further, combining and mixing creative energy has a synergistic effect, enabling you to come up with a breakthrough moment. Your closest bonds get a boost soon. It does see you taking a step back from the demands on your time and exploring an environment that is ripe for personal growth. This light a path towards advancing your social goals. Communication skills get a workout, it prompts you to expand your horizons, and dive into a social environment which uncovers new friendships. More profound soul-searching is also highlighted as being essential during this time. The past has been a valuable learning ground, there is an opportunity ahead to revisit your old stomping ground. It does bring treasured memories to the forefront of your awareness. It enables you to process residual feelings, which may have been limiting your ability to move forward. Surprise news arrives when someone special reaches out over the coming weeks. It does bring lightness into your life.

JANUARY WEEK THREE

This is a nostalgic time that has you thinking back to the past. A distant memory becomes more apparent, it does show a poignant reminder is on its way. Connecting with the past is a valuable way to nurture your spirit. It orientates you towards releasing outworn energy. It adds a bewitching note of nostalgia into your life. This sets the scene for an abundant chapter ahead as you touch base with old friends and valued social groups. You are someone with a beautiful heart, always willing to lend a hand to others. Karma does notice your generosity, you are likely to get a big boost soon. This represents the energy of honor; it brings you an award or an achievement is bestowed upon you. It put your name in lights and draws lucrative new options into your world. Accepting praise does not come easily, being humble and open is the right way to approach this blessing. Things are changing. The past is a valuable tool to reflect on the person you are currently becoming. Essential changes are occurring, which create space for you to nurture your artistic side. A new venture is likely to blossom under your creative vision. It brings confidence out, and this is a trend that is going to occur more often over the coming months. Your status is likely to increase due to your willingness to explore new options.

JANUARY WEEK FOUR

Jupiter goes into Conjunction with the Sun the day after the Full Moon in Leo. Jupiter rules luck, growth, wisdom, and fortune. Life gets a boost from this cosmic alignment, it provides you with ample reason to celebrate. It is a significant moment in your timeline, it activates a positive path towards your goals. As you rise to new heights, excitement rules your vision, it does enable you to advance precious goals. A whirlwind of social activity leaves you feeling happy, things are on the move, and you can feel ready to embrace a new start soon. It is an energizing time which sees you headed out and about. There may be travel involved, you focus on ticking all the boxes, getting your ducks in a row, and being the master of organization. It does bring happy news, and this paves the way for a glorious chapter ahead. A new role makes itself known. This has the potential to radically re-do your goals as you approach life energetically and begin the task of reshaping your vision. A creative project takes flight, it involves writing or working on a highly imaginative area, and enables your talents to be unleashed and set free. It is a time of progress, this sparkling trend that continues to entice and tempt you towards expanding your boundaries. You connect with a friend who puts you in touch with another person who can be of assistance in getting your endeavors to a broader audience.

Mercury Retrograde begins in Aquarius at weeks end, things are heading towards change next month.

FEBRUARY ASTROLOGY

February 2 – Imbolc

February 4 – Last Quarter Moon in Scorpio.

This Moon phase occurs at 17.37 UTC.

February 8 – Mercury at Inferior Conjunction.

The planet Mercury at Inferior Conjunction. This occurs at 14:00 UTC.

February 11 - New Moon in Aquarius.

This phase occurs at 19:06 UTC. This is an excellent time to view galaxies and stars as there is no moonlight to obscure your view of the universe.

February 12 – Chinese New Year (Ox)

February 19 – First Quarter Moon in Taurus.

This Moon phase occurs at 18.47 UTC.

February 21 – Mercury Retrograde ends in Aquarius.

You can now move forward with any delayed plans that you have been putting off due to the Mercury Retrograde phase. Relationships should soon improve as miscommunications are overcome

February 27 - Full Moon in Virgo.

The Moon is on the opposite side of the Earth as the Sun and will be fully illuminated. This phase occurs at 08:17 UTC. This full moon is known as the Full Snow Moon.

FEBRUARY HOROSCOPE

FEBRUARY WEEK ONE

There are a lot of changes coming up, which see restructuring occurring, sifting, and sorting through the options does see goodness rising to the top. You take a step towards your dreams, this directly enables you to stand a good chance of achieving a long-held goal. It does draw excitement into your world when you spot an opportunity to flirt with a complex character who sends electric chemistry directly to your tender spirit. You team up with a refreshing option that enables you to reach for more. This audacity clearly shows you can go in strong, your star is on the rise, and it does take you towards a time of celebration and achievement. It lights the path which offers you something which advances your situation. Praise, recognition, or even a promotion does enable you to feel valued. Pursuing your goals sees you reaching new heights of potential. A surprise message arrives. It does announce an invitation to an event that leaves you feeling optimistic. You are ready to wrap things up and kick back with a more social vibe. Things are changing, there is an undercurrent of potential prepared to emerge, it does create a dramatic shift, and marks the start of a new direction for you. Challenges slip away, and you can look forward to increasing your options moving forward. This is a time that generates invitations, you to dive into a chapter filled with fun, hopes, and dreams. You may discover yourself at a magnificent event that caters to your expectations in the most luxurious manner. It does have you networking within your industry and creates a burst of excitement.

FEBRUARY WEEK TWO

It is a time that sees life turning in your favor. Opportunities to mingle bring you a great advantage, it puts you in the box seat to forge a new friendship. As you embrace lively discussions, you find your charisma is on the rise, it does see your charm shines as your energy sparkles. It does bring opportunities to mingle, it is a season of pure holiday magic. There is time spent at parties, romance is highlighted as being possible. Your friends play a starring role in the season ahead. It does see options arrived to expand your social life. An invitation requires your urgent attention, it could set the stage for an impressive outcome, it has you networking, negotiating a path of catching up with kindred spirits. Romance may come to the forefront as a result of this socializing, it does put you in the right environment to see your charm sparkle. It is a time of increasing opportunity, news arrives, that inspires your imagination. It does place you in the box seat to advance your vision, and sweeping changes may occur as a result of the brainstorming, which occurs soon after. You spend time with friends and associates, it does draw a sense of abundance, and brings warmth and happiness into your life. There are surprises ready to shine in your world, your confidence is on the rise.

FEBRUARY WEEK THREE

Friends play a significant role in your life, it does light a path of friendship, social mingling, and spending time with those who capture your heart. Your hopes and wishes are accented, a vision you seek has been sent to the universe, and is likely to land in your lap with an extraordinary twist. It does help you take a vital step towards advancing your dreams. It is a time that marks the new energy flowing into your world. It is time that sees your energy attracting something which connects you to the past. This captivates your imagination; it warms your spirit, igniting hopes, and wishes. It is a time which is highly social, and being out, mingling in your broader community does have you, meeting new people and connecting with those who become friends. Your life is ready to reach a breathtaking level of potential. It is an essential time that draws harmony into your world. It has you focusing on the ties that bind. This week brings a hilarious episode into your life. It is a return to joy, you get off the merry-go-round of daily demands and spend quality time with someone who captures your inspiration. It has you dreaming about future possibilities and beginning the process of sorting through long-term goals and aspirations. It is a time which enables you to flex your social muscle, invitations to events tempt you out of your usual routine. It does indicate many surprises are coming, it offers you a chance to improve your personal life. You discover that experience supports your vision by providing opportunities for growth. It is a beautiful time that draws an enticing option; it leads to a breathtaking vista of new possibilities.

It is a time that enables you to put your best foot forward into a new area. It sees things take off, and this leads towards exciting developments, You embrace the social expansion, it may also see a new friendship blossom. It all enables you to feel confident about expanding your world. You have an excellent chance to set forth towards new adventures. Knowing that change is vitally important, you are given the stamina and drive to expand your world, and seek experiences that are in alignment with your vision. It does enable creativity to flourish, you crack the code on a fresh chapter of potential when you discover that which inspires your mind. You do lift the lid on a new section. You're on the right path, it does open a gateway, a new role emerges which fits your vision beautifully. It does see you being of service and enables you to spin your magic and bring good outcomes to the table.

News arrives, which leads to an offer that heightens your expectations, it brings you a shift forward. It does lead to a fantastic time of change and growth. The outlook brings a lucky break. This relates to an opportunity that crosses your path, it does come as a bit of a shock at first, but it offers you an excellent chance to upgrade your life. The future begins to look a bit rosier, you feel encouraged and embrace a chapter of advancing your goals. Aiming high is highlighted as improving your fortune. Showing up and following through on your plans takes you further in the chapter head.

March 6 - Mercury Greatest Elongation.

The planet Mercury reaches its greatest elongation of 27.3 degrees from the Sun. If you would like to view Mercury, look for Mercury low in the eastern sky just before sunrise.

March 6 – Last Quarter Moon in Sagittarius.

This Moon phase occurs at 01.30 UTC. –

March 11 – Neptune in Conjunction with the Sun.

The planet Neptune in Conjunction with the Sun. This occurs at 00:00 UTC.

March 13 - New Moon in Pisces.

The New Moon creates space for a new chapter. This phase occurs at 10:21 UTC. This is an excellent time to observe galaxies and stars because there is no moonlight to obscure your view of the universe.

March 20 - Vernal Equinox.

The March equinox takes place at 09:37 UTC. There are equal amounts of day and night throughout the world.

March 21 – First Quarter Moon in Gemini.

This Moon phase occurs at 14.40 UTC.

March 26 - Venus Superior Conjunction.

The planet Venus at Superior Conjunction. This occurs at 06:00 UTC.

March 28 - Full Moon in Libra.

This Moon is on the opposite side of the Earth as the Sun and shall be fully illuminated. This phase occurs at 18:48 UTC. This full moon is known as the Full Worm Moon.

MARCH WEEK ONE

Your life shows impressive progress. The more you focus your energy on nurturing an area, the more it blossoms under your creative vision. It does shine a spotlight on areas that can further your situation. It's your time to shine, success is written in the stars for you ahead. Surprise the news reaches you soon, it is a spectacular breakthrough to a new phase of personal growth. A radical makeover arrives to see you rise towards success. There are options on the table, which enable you to progress your vision in the best possible way. Finishing up the workload creates space for an abundant chapter to rejuvenate your spirit. It does bring supportive energy, spending time with your closest ties, does see you benefiting from a beautiful home environment. It is an energizing time which presents you with new options. You may discover a gift lands in your lap, this has you unwrap a new chapter and offers you a role you had previously discounted. Approaching a life energetically, you expand your world and embrace a fresh flow of potential. Things are shifting forward, it does see you involved in an area which draws happiness, this becomes an enormous focus for your attention moving forward. It is a time which brings startling news, it can see travel involved. You are invited to a grand event surrounded by warm and bubbly people. Many are your friends, but there are also new people to get to know. You find yourself surrounded by inspiring types that offer thoughtful and contemplative dialogue. It takes place in an exceptional setting, it does set the stage for your imagination to take flight.

MARCH WEEK TWO

There is support coming from your more full circle, touching base with friends and social connections to help provide you with a framework of valuable guidance and advice. Something is troubling you with your current situation, it does become more evident this week. A big part of wanting to create change is knowing that you can branch out on your own, and feel supported by those around you. Your current trajectory is not likely to change unless you create a move towards your goals. It is a time of integrating your thoughts and feelings about recent events. As you process and deal with your emotions surrounding the challenges you have overcome, you release energy, which has held you back. This process can feel slow, don't try and push against the flow of emotional awareness. Things are likely to be in flux, you will find a shift forward occurs after doing this inner work. You soon find it is an easier time to navigate than it has been in previous months. It puts you in the middle of an abundant chapter, and it does ease the pressure, this sees communication improving. It does hearten your spirit and gives you the strength to start thinking about new goals and plans. You have an open road of potential before you, your free and willing heart is ready for a journey that inspires your mind. A special memory has the power to transform your outlook, it brings a beautiful new perspective. Looking back, you can understand the true meaning of unconditional love. You draw harmony into your world and can embrace being enveloped by the bonds which capture the feelings of love and affection. The past is a time you can treasure, and it does bring a passport towards future success. The past rules your heart, it gives you a solid basis from which to grow your world.

MARCH WEEK THREE

It is currently a time where you have the golden touch, it does increase your magnetism, and lets you embrace a more social environment. The good news is that you can create space to nurture your creativity, an option arrives, which leads to a venture that brings in plenty of excitement. It underscores your ability to improve your circumstances. You are in a time of transition, and this brings with it more support from the universe. Now, the great thing about this time is that it lands you in an environment that is ripe for exploring, it enables you to embark on a new adventure. Important news coming, as you are close to a breakthrough in your personal life. It does see that months ahead beautifully align with your vision. There are going to be options to circulate over the coming weeks; this launches you into an area that draws something new into your life. The timing is terrific, it marks a significant moment in your life, and it does see you having the courage and drive to expand your horizons. You discover that there is a highly social aspect ahead, and it does enable your radiance to shine. It does suggest you attend a beautiful party, and this event provides you with the right environment to see a situation blossom. You mingle with successful, interesting people at this event, and it does see you moving in alignment with your vision. It is an enchanting time, one which offers you a fantastic chance to move forward in your personal life. A conversation occurs, which stays with you long after the night has finished.

MARCH WEEK FOUR

There are some changes ahead. You may have been feeling progress in your life has been limited, an area which has impeded the flow of potential is set to be lifted. Once this restriction is resolved, you discover new options flow beautifully into your world. It really sets the ball rolling on a new chapter, and exciting area lights up with exciting possibilities. There are encouraging signs that things are shifting forward. This is going to shine a light on new potential, it highlights increasing harmony, and it does help you move ahead with your goals. You've been through plenty of changes recently, it's given you insight into where you are headed, and how you need to approach things to get where you are going. This is the perfect time to spend with friends and your more full social circle. It does introduce a busy time where invitations arrive, meetings crop up, and you may even be invited to take a short trip to an exotic destination. It does have an uplifting effect on your personal life, this releases doubts, and lights up a very inspiring path. This is a time that shines a light on the areas of harmony, joy, and connection. It does see progress being made, which connects you with friends and links you to invitations and events which have you feeling excited. You can dive in and embrace a chapter that sparkles with possibilities.

April 4 – Last Quarter Moon in Capricorn.

This Moon phase occurs at 10.02 UTC.

April 12 - New Moon in Aries.

The New Moon phase occurs at 2:31 UTC. This is an excellent time to observe galaxies and stars because there is no moonlight visible.

April 19 – Mercury at Superior Conjunction.

The planet Mercury at Superior Conjunction. This occurs at 02:00 UTC.

April 20 – First Quarter Moon in Leo.

This Moon phase occurs at 06.59 UTC.

April 22, 23 - Lyrids Meteor Shower.

The Lyrids meteor shower runs each year from April 16-25. This meteor shower peaks on the night of the 22nd and the morning of the 23rd. These meteors can produce bright dust trails that last for several seconds.

April 27 - Full Moon in Scorpio, Supermoon.

The Moon is on the opposite side of the Earth as the Sun and will be completely illuminated. Full Pink Moon. It's the first of three supermoons for 2021. This occurs at 03:31 UTC. The Moon will be at its closest approach to the Earth and may look slightly larger and brighter than usual.

April 30 – Uranus in Conjunction with the Sun.

The planet Uranus in Conjunction with the Sun. This occurs at 21:00 UTC.

APRIL WEEK ONE

You may have been working too hard, slowing down, exploring your options, let's you discover a little worn path which offers you a chance to rejuvenate and grow your spirit. Friends surround you with opportunities to mingle, it leads to a happy season of catching up with kindred spirits. Additionally, you connect with a path that brings happiness, optimism, and potential. It is a route that draws excitement into your world. This is a time of freedom and adventure, an exciting new path opens which beckons and shifts your focus towards expanding your life. It does leave you feeling excited about the potential possible. Merging with happiness, it adds up to the high time of listening to your intuition. It does bring significant movement, which draws essential changes. A secret is revealed by someone who needs to get something off their chest. It has been an edgy time. This is set to improve. A necessary recalibration takes place, it does bring new potential. The festive season holds plenty of surprises, it enables any unstable foundations to become more grounded, and goal orientated, this heightens the security possible. There is a celebratory atmosphere that brings exciting news. It is a time of happiness, optimism, and joy ahead. It is a time that lights up refreshing options for you. You feel ready to embrace the changes ahead. It does chart a magical course towards improving your situation. It's seeing expansion occurring in your social life.

APRIL WEEK TWO

The New Moon in Aries packs a nugget of wisdom. There is energy under the surface, currently hidden from view, but will soon be discovered. It does point a path forward's towards an exceptional chapter. There is lovely creative energy at the basis of this time, it does enable you to plot a course towards achieving a spectacular level of advancement. You're ready to climb the ladder towards success. The wheel is turning in your favor, this sees opportunities arriving, it does enable you to expand your horizons and set off on a new adventure. It is a journey that reveals an enticing bevy of new potential. Moving out of your usual routine, you negotiate the path ahead with an open heart, this begins your hero's journey into uncharted territory. It does draw you to a surprising path which expands your life in ways you don't realize is possible. It sets off a beautiful cascade of new options that build your talents and add to your repertoire of skills. It places you precisely where you need to be to accept an offer that crosses your path. Life sparkles when unexpected good news reaches you soon. It does bring lightness and enthusiasm into your world. It strikes an interesting note, as it brings a refreshing option for you to contemplate. This boost may even further advance your situation by transitioning you to an area that has the potential to grow your life. It is a path of hope and happiness that glitters with creative options. It is a time which brings good news and could open a new chapter in your life. You discover that events work in your favor. You have plenty of support and can feel confident about passing this inspection. It is a time that brings surprise news and may lead to an offer for you to consider. Try not to focus on uncertainty, keep positive, and resonate with the highest frequency possible. News ahead becomes the source of great happiness.

APRIL WEEK THREE

Mercury at Superior conjunction this week sees you reaching a crossroads, it does bring essential changes and leads to a chapter that opens a new path. This is a journey you embrace, it does give you options that warm your spirit. It represents following your heart and going after your dreams. It is an environment that taps into your need for deeper connection; expanding your life is a trend that carries you forward towards greener pastures. The significant change is possible, it brings a critical moment which advances your vision. Staying right to your heart does light a brilliant path of what is possible. It takes your situation to an entirely new level, it brings passion, courage, and a drive to follow through in your aspirations. As you express this energy outward, it does connect you to a transformational environment. Taking time to contemplate your strategy may lead to a reconfiguration of your vision. It does land you in an exciting landscape, and some sort of sign arrives to guide your decision-making process. It brings remarkable change, there is a theme of self-development emerging, you begin to focus on growing your soul. It draws spontaneous energy and sweet surprises into your world. A bonanza of refreshing opportunity awaits an open heart. The stage is set for an incredible chapter of exciting new options. It does initiate significant change, you see signs that you can advance your life and begin developing a path that inspires your mind. The fantastic bonus is how this positive energy spills over into other areas of your life.

APRIL WEEK FOUR

The Full Moon in Scorpio is a Supermoon. It sees new options flowing into your world soon. This is a time which draws abundance into your world, it does give you plenty to look forward to. A sense of déjà vu brings a sentimental theme, it does have you reflecting on the past, and exploring your life through the lens of treasured memories. It is a time that brings a social element, this is wonderful as it connects you with your broader community. It is a time that offers a bounty of opportunity. It does build on your life and put you in the right mindset to plan towards a prestigious goal. A unique project you get involved with progressing draws inspiration. It sets the scene for future growth, and it aligns you towards making the most of your talents. It may even bring a landmark moment that culminates in a breakthrough. It is a time which draws new experiences, you discover a chance to socialize, it brings you in alignment with others who have similar interests. You thrive in this natural environment, lively discussions draw unexpected news. Attending a gathering of kindred spirits, lets your ideas loose, and brings your creativity to a high point. It does put you in a position of influence, and you garner the attention of another.

Next month is going to transform your life on many levels, you go after your goals, a big focus is on self-development, the lifestyle changes you make, draw dividends. Additionally, a new area blossom in your life brings great excitement and joy. It is your time to shine, and you are pleased with the results of your hard work. Change is not easy, but you will be so happy that you took the plunge and went after your dreams.

May 3 – Last Quarter Moon in Aquarius.

This Moon phase occurs at 17.50 UTC.

May 6, 7 - Eta Aquarids Meteor Shower.

The Eta Aquarids meteor shower runs annually from April 19 to May 28. It peaks this year on the night of May 6 and the morning of May 7.

May 11 - New Moon in Taurus.

This phase occurs at 19:00 UTC. The new moon phase is a brilliant time to observe galaxies and stars because there is no moonlight visible.

March 17 - Mercury Greatest Eastern Elongation.

The planet Mercury reaches its greatest eastern elongation of 22 degrees from the Sun. If you would like to view Mercury, look for the Mercury low in the sky just after sunset. This planetary phase occurs at 06.00 UTC.

May 19 – First Quarter Moon in Virgo.

This Moon phase occurs at 19.13 UTC.

May 26 - Full Moon in Sagittarius, Supermoon.

This phase occurs at 11:14 UTC. Full Flower Moon. It's the second of three supermoons for 2021. The Moon will be at its closest approach to the Earth and may look slightly larger and brighter than usual.

May 26 – Total Lunar Eclipse in Sagittarius.

A total lunar eclipse occurs when the Moon passes completely through the Earth's dark shadow or umbra. During this type of eclipse, the Moon gradually gets more mysterious and then take on a rusty or blood red color. This eclipse occurs at 11:19 UTC.

May 29 – Mercury Retrograde begins in Gemini.

During a retrograde period, it isn't the right time to move forward in any practical venture. Be prepared for misunderstandings and miscommunications to be prevalent.

MAY WEEK ONE

You are now at the point when you're ready to wipe the slate clean, heal the past, and become an open book available for new chapters. It does build your vision, it creates a direct link between your aspirations, and achieving the happiness you desire. New options dance in your mind, your creativity heightens and becomes a valuable tool, enabling you to create a pathway towards abundance.

The stars reveal a fresh start, which leaves you bursting with excitement. It does draw a joyful chapter, it brings benefits that are rare and bountiful. This glorious news appears in your life to expand your awareness and inspire your imagination. It does have you plotting a course towards rebooting your vision and creating the changes necessary that help you harness the energy of manifestation. It is a time that enables you to close the door on an area that feels finished with. As you gather your thoughts, you begin to plot a course towards achieving a new vision. It is an ideal time to contemplate the path ahead and organize your goals. Taking steps to plan the strategy lifts your spirits as it shows you that things are coming together. It does bring new options rolling into your life soon. A message you receive soon has you feeling excited, it brings a surprise, and draws a new inspiration into your world. It adds magic to this holiday season and gives you a fantastic reason to celebrate. A theme of abundance is emerging, this has you feeling positive about expanding your life and exploring new options.

MAY WEEK TWO

Stargazing under the Taurus New Moon this week lifts you up if you feel down. It is a beautiful thing for you to call upon the universe to help; the cosmos is more than willing to be the wind beneath your wings. In fact, essential changes are currently configuring in the background of your life, these will make themselves known to you soon, and it does draw more happiness into your world. A sweet surprise lands in your lap. It opens productive conversations, you discover a social environment becomes a focal point. It does bring new information and experiences, you open your eyes to the bounty of potential waiting at the periphery of your vision. A collaboration you get involved with does draw abundance into your world. Spending time with kindred spirits brings joy, you scout out a path which offers a real sense of connection. You receive communication soon, which is especially poignant. It does bring a powerful moment and lights a way forward. It brings a more social environment, it has you thinking about the potential possible. As you begin to plot a course towards achieving your goals, you benefit from your willingness to step out of your comfort zone and draw in new experiences. There is some exciting activity afoot in your social life coming. You soon ring in new opportunities; this takes you towards a trend that enables further growth is achievable. It brings a time that offers you new possibilities, it also blends well with your current situation, so it doesn't feel like an uncomfortable evolution, it brings new experiences and more prosperous social life. This creates the fresh start you have been seeking.

MAY WEEK THREE

Mercury reaches greatest elongation from the Sun this week. This reveals that you are positioned to advance your life. It centers on developing a project that brings magical potential into your world. Before moving forward, it may be helpful to backtrack and contemplate what needs to be released. It is a time that gives you a chance to pull back, catch your breath, and think about healing and rejuvenation. Secret news is revealed, which draws clarity. It enables you to gain a deeper understanding of an area that had been problematic.

Necessary change arrives to guide your progress forward. It multiplies the potential possible, and this aligns you towards a path that grows your vision. It does harness your valuable talents, and delivers a beautiful bounty, the more you go after your dreams, the higher you can advance your life. Luck and good fortune are your company on this journey forward. It is a time which amplifies your potential, an influx of new options leave you feeling starry-eyed. You find it is a hectic time, which is quite motivating and lively. It does let you launch your vision and build a stairway towards achieving a substantial goal. You may receive unexpected yet thrilling news. It seems a trend is occurring, a fantastic theme of abundance is ready to blossom into your world. Exciting news reaches you, it has you diving into a busy time. You invite the hub of commotion into your world. It does draw active and energetic options that inspire your mind. It initiates positive change, you embrace the expansion, your taste for new experiences enables you to take a leap of faith into the unknown. It does see change arriving, lots of social activity shines a light on an abundant chapter.

MAY WEEK FOUR

This week delivers a plethora of cosmic activity. There is a full moon in Sagittarius, which is also a super moon, and on the same night, we also have a total lunar eclipse. This is a triple magnifying event. But be warned, three days later Mercury retrograde begins in Gemini, this is the mule kick that may just knock you sideways if you're not aware, that it is coming. So what does all this mean for your life? The triple combo event on Wednesday is going to bring up a lot of unsettling energy, it invites you to dig deeper and reveal what has been affecting your life negatively. There is a sense of illumination of what is hidden, and it can encourage you to make a great decision as you may feel at a crossroads; however, it's too early to do this with Mercury retrograde poised to strike. Use this time to think about the areas that need work. You are going through an unsettling chapter, it can have you re-evaluating many elements of your life. It is, in fact, a transition towards a new path, embrace the open field of possibilities, and prepare to experiment, get creative, and enjoy the journey. You discover further information about the past, it does bring clarity, and you gain a deeper understanding of areas that have troubled you previously.

You may discover that someone wants to share their thoughts with you, and this person does offer support and guidance. It draws harmony and abundance into your life and does pave the way forward to an unobstructed chapter of potential. It is a time that brings blessings and joy. There is support in your wider community; you can appreciate the benefits which emerge from this time.

June 2 – Last Quarter Moon in Pisces.

This Moon phase occurs at 07.24 UTC.

June 10 - New Moon in Gemini.

This moon phase occurs at 10:53 UTC. This is an excellent time to observe galaxies and stars because there is little moonlight to obstruct your view.

June 10 – Annual Solar Eclipse.

An annular solar eclipse occurs when the Moon is too far away from the Earth to completely cover the Sun, it results in a ring of light around the dark Moon. The Sun's corona isn't visible during an annular eclipse. This solar eclipse is visible in eastern Russia, the Arctic Ocean, western Greenland, and Canada. A partial eclipse will be visible in the northeastern United States, Europe, and most of Russia. This eclipse occurs at 10.42 UTC.

June 11 – Mercury at Inferior Conjunction.

The planet Mercury at Inferior Conjunction. This occurs at 01:00 UTC.

June 18 – First Quarter Moon in Libra.

This Moon phase occurs at 03.54 UTC.

June 21 - June Solstice.

The June solstice occurs at 03:32 UTC. The North Pole will be tilted toward the Sun, which, having reached its northernmost position in the sky, will be over the Tropic of Cancer at 23.44 degrees north latitude. This heralds the first day of summer (summer solstice) in the Northern Hemisphere, the summer solstice is considered one of the most important times of the year for many traditional cultures.

June 22 – Mercury Retrograde ends in Gemini.

You can now move forward with any delayed plans that you have been putting off due to the Mercury Retrograde phase. Relationships should soon improve as miscommunications are overcome

June 24 - Full Moon in Capricorn, Supermoon.

The Moons will be completely illuminated. This moon phase occurs at 18:40 UTC. Full Strawberry Moon. This is the last of three supermoons for 2021. The Moon will be at its closest approach to the Earth and may look slightly larger and brighter than usual.

JUNE WEEK ONE

You have the stamina to overcome hurdles and stay on top of things during this Mercury Retrograde phase. Time is healing in itself. A situation that is causing you in issue will be considerably softened by allowing things to flow gently forward. There is some big news coming, which shines a light on a positive chapter. It is a time where you may feel restless, a sense of disenchantment brings up the energy for seeking new adventures. It's a time which brings changes, it is your time to shine. You discover an area which beckons, this draws a sense of excitement, you are ready to expand your life and embrace more freedom in your world. It's also a time of surprises, a secret is revealed, this gives you clarity into the path ahead. You are ready to pull back the lever and open a pathway that ignites your inspiration. Things are going to turn around, it does take a willingness to expand your life and move out of your comfort zone. A fabulous change is coming, keep forging ahead, and an innovative solution is around the corner. Taking time to build the path ahead carefully and with diligence and perseverance, offers you a chance to really make the most of this week. You are growing your life, and something is coming soon, which becomes a source of great happiness for you. It does look indeed that the happy chapter is arriving soon. It connects you to your vision.

The New Moon in Gemini combines with an annular solar eclipse, this sees change ahead for you. It does bring a big moment, these changes shake up your home environment, you discover that news reaches you that expands your life, and helps you go after a long-awaited goal. It is a joyous time that packs a powerful punch of potential. A remarkable change is coming, and these alterations partner you with a happy environment from which to grow your vision. A path of hope and happiness glitters with gold. It transitions you towards a chapter that is luxurious, festive, and undoubtedly memorable. You are in sync with your vision, it draws transformation and invites advancement to your life. This is a time which also brings surprises and good news; it let you open a new chapter in the book of your life. Events unfold in your favor, allowing you to venture forth, expanding your horizons. This is a time where you grow your career path. It does lead to an expansive outcome that offers you room to flex your talents and achieve a stellar result. You shine a light on advancing your situation, through your dedication and perseverance, you come out on top. Your innovative thinking is inspired, it's guiding you towards an endeavor that offers you room to grow your situation. It does turn into a big project, this is the perfect outlet to flex your talents and expand your life. It sees you creating space to nurture your gifts, and it enables you to grow your life beautifully. Your efforts are rewarded with a bountiful result; it could even head right off the chart with the effects possible. Change is flowing into your life. It does bring success and enables you to plot a course towards a vision that encompasses a great deal of growth. It is a magical time to think about the future, and this takes the edge off worrying about progression.

JUNE WEEK THREE

The June 21st Solstice at weeks end is an ideal time to pause and reflect on your goals. There is a new chapter coming which beckons and calls your name. Your quest to improve your situation draws dividends, it's a time when creative ideas excite your mind, and you discover a path that brings benefits. It does see moving out of your usual routine, it's the perfect time to shine a light on adventure and freedom. The changes ahead bring you positive results, it inspires your vision to grow. You can plot a course towards obtaining a substantial goal. A new assignment pours into your life. It is the right kind of project to sink your teeth into. You attract new options, and this leads to a rush of activity. Overseeing the demands on your time does heighten your organizational abilities. You attract new prospects, which become a significant turning point. It delivers a rare and beautiful path, bringing gifts and luck into your world. You are ready to grow your situation and advance your vision. It is a time of lucky surprises, this lights the way forward. It does see you setting up a new venture, working on your life has you exceptionally busy. Investigating leads draws powerful options, it does bring potential worth developing. It sets in motion the right type of projects to inspire your mind. It is a wonderfully motivating factor that enables you to plan ahead and build your goals correctly.

JUNE WEEK FOUR

Mercury Retrograde ends this week. This draws harmony into your world and brings lively and surprising news. A gathering you attend brings a powerful moment of joy. The stage is set, everything is lining up for you. Things are going to arrive, which initiates change, it gives you a sign that you indeed are on the right path. As the world turns in your favor, you embrace the effects it has on your situation. It does bring a busy time, a lively surprise comes out of nowhere to bless your life with happy news. Surprise, information ignites a time of inspiration, learning, and growth. It opens a chapter where you can expand your vision, you discover things come together with a flourish. If you have been stuck with a sense of uncertainty recently, this new energy brings a magical element that replenishes your spirit and transitions you towards an expansive chapter. It does have you entertaining ideas that draw excitement into your world.

You lift the lid on a new chapter of potential. It does draw marvelous changes into your world, it highlights the enchanting atmosphere which dazzles with new potential. This aligns you towards developing a lively vision and connected. It does draw gatherings, events, and meaningful conversations. It shines a light on developing a bond with one who understands your needs. You are ready to kick back and take in new adventures. It does see a magical time, which is a transition towards a freedom-loving chapter. It is a lucky time that brings magic news into your world. It does have a fantastic effect on your social life and enables you to bond well with the people who you feel a secure connection with.

July 1 – Last Quarter Moon in Aries.

This Moon phase occurs at 21.11 UTC.

July 4 - Mercury at Greatest Western Elongation.

The planet Mercury reaches greatest western elongation of 20.6 degrees from the Sun. If you would like to view Mercury, look for Mercury low in the eastern sky just before sunrise. This planetary phase occurs at 20.00 UTC.

July 10 - New Moon in Cancer.

The New Moon draws rebirth and new energy. This moon phase occurs at 01:17 UTC. This is an excellent time to observe galaxies and stars because there is no moonlight visible.

July 17 – First Quarter Moon in Libra.

This Moon phase occurs at 10.11 UTC.

July 24 - Full Moon in Aquarius.

The Moon is located on the opposite side of the Earth as the Sun and will be fully illuminated. This phase occurs at 02:37 UTC. This full moon is known as Full Buck Moon.

July 28, 29 - Delta Aquarids Meteor Shower.

The Delta Aquarids meteor shower peaks on the night of July 28 and the morning of July 29. The first quarter moon may block many of the fainter meteors this year. You should still be able to view some brighter ones. Best viewing will be at a dark vista after midnight. Meteors radiate from the constellation Aquarius but can appear anywhere in the sky.

July 31 – Last Quarter Moon in Taurus.

This Moon phase occurs at 13.16 UTC.

JULY WEEK ONE

Mercury at Greatest elongation this week brings unusual vibrations. Things are shifting for you, and these sands can feel unstable. An offer reaches you soon, and you question the path ahead. Focusing on releasing doubts, you make a decision from your gut. It's a big step forward, it brings a new level of excitement into your world. Change is around you this July. A decision is made soon. It clears the path and enables you to make progress on a lofty goal. It does set the stage for a bounty of potential to emerge in your life. You are hungry to expand your life, it opens a prosperous path which paves the way for a new way of life. You discover an area you nurture becomes a project you feel passionate about. You do lift the lid on a new chapter. You are on the right path, it does open a gateway, a new role emerges which fits your vision beautifully. It does see you being of service and enables you to spin your magic and bring good outcomes to the table. It is an ideal time to plan the path forward.

You are ready to grow your situation and advance your goals. Soon, you receive relevant news, it does offer a high octane path where you can develop your vision. It draws essential changes into your world, which strongly favors growth. It helps you create long term security, and this is the improvement that brings blessings into your life.

JULY WEEK TWO

The New Moon in Cancer this week signifies a new beginning. This sees you successfully emerge from a cocoon where you have sheltered your creativity recently. Life becomes a whirlwind of potential; it sweeps through your life and heightens your available options. You are attracting new prospects, a rush of activity is coming to, which brings abundance to your world. It seems you reach the pinnacle, which enables you a fast overview of potential pathways. Taking time to contemplate your goals does allow you to pinpoint the right direction to head towards. There is a positive influence coming, which provides you with a sense of rejuvenation. This is a time that creates change and opportunity, it offers many surprises, and does bring good news. An unexpected arrival lands in your lap soon. It kicks off a chapter of new projects and assignments; it does bring magic into your surroundings, and this transitions you towards a time that advances your vision. Amplifying your talents grows your potential.

This is a time that brings surprising news, it does reflect a vision you have sent out to the universe. Something you have wanted dearly does spring to life. It gives you a moment worth celebrating. Your situation is set to advance, and this brings key developments that leave you feeling excited. It is your time to shine soon. A new trend begins in your life soon, it sees you pouring your energy into a situation which draws blessings into your world. An area you focus your energy on will draw improvement to your life. It is a chapter that brings joy and harmony into focus. Improving your experience draws warmth and good fortune to your landscape.

JULY WEEK THREE

It's a perfect time to contemplate your vision, streamlining your goals enables you to remove the deadwood, and focus on progression. There is much to be excited about, your life is ready to brim with new activities and projects. Using a methodical approach, you set up the systems that keep your situation moving forward. Refining your talents lets you be more efficient and productive. There is an assignment coming which elevates your career potential. Things are on the move for you, it does draw a plethora of new options into your world. Your creative thinking blends beautifully with your goals. It sees you feeling energized, you can achieve a great deal of growth. Taking proactive measures creates enriching pathways towards abundance. It brings an industrious and productive chapter, which leaves you feeling refreshed and happy. Improving your life is something you are ready to dive into. Becoming serious about advancing your situation, does set the scene for a productive chapter of growth. This is a great time to venture out of your comfort zone and discover a path that enables you to grow your talents. Essential changes are coming, which tweak this journey of advancement.

Abundance hovers at the periphery of your life. It does come into view soon, and this lines you up with a path that brings joy. It gives you something special to pour your energy into. This relates to your home environment, it sees a dream you hold dear come into focus. You can reach for the stars, this begins a chapter that sets off a new beginning in your personal life. Some developments initiate positive change. It does draw a powerful path that sees essential changes arriving. It attracts abundance and does have you feeling encouraged by the signs which tempt you forward.

JULY WEEK FOUR

The magic of the Full Moon arrives to put you in manifestation mode. It sees an outpouring of creativity is possible, an endeavor you focus on does take flight, you watch your ideas blossom. As your imagination and creative thinking are heightened, it does powerfully shape your vision. Planning the path ahead lights up a journey worth exploring. The surprising news is coming, there is plenty of excitement around the corner. This is a time which brightens your life, things are looking very positive, it does see advancement is possible soon. With so much potential around the corner, it does have you thinking about the future. Plotting a course towards your vision does align you correctly. It turns the tables in your favor. An opportunity tailor-made for your life is drawing near. This is a magical time to head out and mingle. It does see you meeting new people and attending events that offer excitement. Happy news flows into your life; this is a theme that lightens your mood and sets you off in pursuit of a personal goal. Communication with others lights a favorable path forward. You receive a notification which brings excitement, it touches your heart and elevates your spirit. News arrives, which brings a lovely surprise, it enables you to plot a course towards an elevated option. This is a lucky break, as it harnesses the energy of happiness. It may even lead to a breakthrough moment. This week will be one of the sweetest, most joyful times you've had recently. It does resonate with a sentimental theme, it draws healing into your world and enables you to balance your emotions, and feel supported to expand your world. It is a beautiful temple which is capable of rebooting your life and rejuvenating your spirit. This powerful alchemy transitions you towards new goals.

August 1 – Mercury at Superior Conjunction.

The planet Mercury at Superior Conjunction. This planetary event occurs at 14:00 UTC.

August 2 - Saturn at Opposition.

The beautiful ringed planet Saturn will be at its nearest approach to Earth and will be illuminated by the Sun. This planetary event occurs at 05:00 UTC.

August 8 - New Moon in Leo.

This moon phase occurs at 13:50 UTC. This is an excellent time to observe galaxies and stars because there is no moonlight to obstruct the view. A new chapter awaits an open heart.

August 12, 13 - Perseids Meteor Shower.

The Perseids meteor shower runs each year from July 17 to August 24. It peaks this year on the night of August 12 and the morning of August 13. The Perseids meteor shower is usually excellent viewing as the meteors are so bright and numerous. The moon sets early in the evening, leaving dark skies for what could be a unique show. The best viewing is from after midnight.

August 15 – First Quarter Moon in Scorpio.

This Moon phase occurs at 15.20 UTC.

August 19 - Jupiter at Opposition.

The Giant planet Jupiter will be at its nearest approach to Earth and will be at it's brightest. This planetary event occurs at 23:00 UTC.

August 22 - Full Moon in Aquarius, Blue Moon.

The Full Moon draws clarity and illumination. This phase occurs at 12:02 UTC. Full Sturgeon Moon. This year it is also a blue moon. This event only happens on average once every 2.7 years, giving rise to the term, "once in a blue moon." There are three full moons in each season of the year. But as full moons occur every 29.53 days, occasionally a season contains 4 full moons. The additional full moon of the season is known as a blue moon.

August 30 – Last Quarter Moon in Gemini.

This Moon phase occurs at 07.13 UTC.

AUGUST HOROSCOPE

AUGUST WEEK ONE

Saturn at opposition this week brings the energy that is diligent, persevering, reliable, stable, patient. It lets you possess the ability to concentrate. Life overflows with happy surprises, it does enable a shift forward. This new beginning brings terrific opportunities, you set forth on an adventure that offers room to grow your life. It is a powerful chapter that initiates a time of prime chances. There is a great deal of change seeking to emerge in your life, you're allowed to share ideas with an influencer, it does help open the path ahead, your creativity is on the rise, this motivates you to move out of your comfort zone. The more you communicate your vision, the better you shape your future potential. A course or learning endeavor is in the stars for you. The universe is creating a lovely shift, this is encouraging news, there is a change of perspective. The emphasis is placed squarely on drawing abundance into your world. Warmth and good luck are rising; it helps you express your thoughts and ideas to another. Being more self-expressive and in alignment with your vision becomes a huge focus for you. Taking a step back does draw a broader perspective, it offers a compelling opportunity, you may be feeling impatient to see progress, and seek to push things forward with abandon. This is not the time to haste or rush into significant change. It does highlight better communication flowing into your world, this enables you to regain balance, and it does influence a more abundant chapter which offers you room to expand your life.

AUGUST WEEK TWO

The New Moon in Leo this week begins a new chapter. It is a time that sees you going in strong and able to plan your goals for the next while. A quest you undertake offers substantial progression; it is a journey that takes flight and sees you elevate your situation. It does bring benefits, an enjoyable aspect of this path is your ability to grow your vision and adapt to your environment.

It is a time which has you reaching for the stars, you discover that dreams can come true. Your luck is turning, fortune favors the bold, it brings new energy into your world. You are ready to heal the past and move towards a path which rejuvenates and renews your spirit. If you have been thinking about the changes to make, keep contemplating your options, there is a sector that is going to draw your attention. It brings a lot of social activities, places to see, and new people to befriend. It is the change that you have been seeking. Life hits a high point soon, it does draw the right note of excitement into your world. It is a sweet and joyful time, and this supports your emotional well-being, it does see you mingling with people that are compatible with your life. As you improve your situation, you touch down on an environment that nurtures your spirit. It draws security and positions you ideally to advance your life. You are in the perfect place to cook up a storm and use creative thinking to plot an unusual path forward. Something special is coming, it has you feeling enthusiastic about the future. Joy and happiness pervade your world, this is an extraordinary time of drawing abundance, a surprise lands on your doorstep, which has a wonderfully positive effect on your outlook. A long-awaited moment is drawing near.

AUGUST WEEK THREE

You have an uncanny ability to navigate complexities and come out on top. Innovative and creative thinking are used to gain a definite advantage over the coming months. Some of the chaos which has been swirling around your life dissipates, it no longer stirs your emotions, you know that change is on the horizon, it illuminates a path that helps you chart your course towards smoother waters. You are ready for change. This is a time that brings a plethora of options to contemplate. It does fill your life with energy, courage, and enthusiasm. An opportunity arrives that gives you a significant advantage. It is an ideal time to launch your vision, and it does seem you are negotiating a path that enables you to build new foundations. As you crack open this chapter, there is an emphasis on achieving robust growth. It is a time that sees a powerful shift occurring; this contributes to new options, it sets a trend that brings growth, and this helps you go after your goals. It enables you to see progress occurring reasonably quickly. Advancing your situation blazes a new path forward. News also arrives unexpectedly, it sparkles with an offer you can't resist. It is a time of goodness and brilliance that shines a positive beam of optimism over your world.

AUGUST WEEK FOUR

The Full Moon in Aquarius at the beginning of this week is also a rare blue moon. This brings unsettling energy that can make you feel restless and uncomfortable, this is to shake you out of complacency and really take a good look at where you are headed, and what your current trajectory is. It can be challenging to see the path ahead when you face a fork in the road. Choosing harmony over your ambitions draws a happier environment. Paying attention to life's synchronicity provides you with the intuitive guidance you can count on. A soul-stirring vision emerges through your willingness to contemplate innovative options. Moving beyond recent restrictions highlights a time of movement and discovery ahead. You reveal a path that offers rapid growth. This illuminates a compelling way forward. It is a shift that enables you to focus on building your life and advancing your vision. Things are ready to turn a corner, it does spark a chapter of new potential. The intensity of past issues are released, the future brings a new dawn. It has you seeing your situation from a broader perspective. Opening your heart reveals options that draw abundance. You gain peace as you gently unfurl new foundations that bring stability. An air of inspiration ignites creativity. You benefit from new ideas and thought processes which get the ball rolling on creating a path toward success. A burst of inspiration sets the stage for future progress, you can plan to advance your situation. It soon sees you heading in the right direction, new options emerge which support your vision.

September 7 - New Moon in Virgo.

The Moon is on the same side of the Earth as the Sun and will not be visible in the night sky. This phase occurs at 00:52 UTC. This is an excellent time to observe galaxies and stars because there is no moonlight visible.

September 13 – First Quarter Moon in Sagittarius.

This Moon phase occurs at 20.39 UTC.

September 14 - Neptune at Opposition.

The giant blue planet will be at its closest approach to Earth, and its face will be illuminated by the Sun. This event occurs at 08:00 UTC.

September 14 - Mercury at Greatest Eastern Elongation.

The planet Mercury reaches greatest eastern elongation of 23.8 degrees from the Sun. This event occurs at 04:00 UTC. This is the best time to view Mercury. Look for the planet low in the western sky just after sunset.

September 20 - Full Moon in Pisces.

The Moon is on the opposite side of the Earth as the Sun, and its face will be fully illuminated. This phase occurs at 23:55 UTC. Full Corn Moon. This moon is also known as the Harvest Moon. The Harvest Moon is the full moon that occurs closest to the September equinox each year.

September 22 - September Equinox.

The 2021 September equinox occurs at 19:21 UTC. The Sun shines directly on the equator, creating equal amounts of day and night throughout the world. This is also autumnal equinox in the northern hemisphere and is considered a significant zodiac event for many traditional cultures.

September 27 – Mercury Retrograde begins in Libra.

During a retrograde period, it isn't the right time to move forward in any practical venture. Be prepared for misunderstandings and miscommunications to be more prevalent.

September 29 – Last Quarter Moon in Cancer.

This Moon phase occurs at 01.57 UTC.

SEPTEMBER HOROSCOPE

SEPTEMBER WEEK ONE

Striking out in a new area, you take tentative steps to improve your situation, while things may feel stuck, you are slowly gaining pace. Before long, you discover you can hit your stride and successfully emerge from the doldrums, which have sheltered your creativity in recent times. Breaking free of limitations drives the metamorphosis. It takes you towards a more adventurous and energizing chapter. You grow your talents and dive deep into uncharted territory. It is a time which cracks open the potential possible, you go through a time of reflecting about the past and integrating the lessons learned, a gateway opens towards a brighter future, you shift towards a new beginning. It does lead to some upgrades, these improvements help you move in alignment with your truth. Being authentic about what you need and want in your life does have a profound effect on your emotional welfare; it leads to a prosperous time that draws happiness into your world. An option ahead makes itself known, this is highly rejuvenating, it does lift your energy and creates a fantastic sense of excitement. New ideas bring a burst of optimism, it brings inspired thinking. Movement and discovery arrive, the pace gains momentum, and this marks a chapter which puts your talents front and center. It does help you use your gifts to create an environment that draws abundance. It culminates in a role that inspires your mind. It's a huge turning point, it harnesses your innovation and creativity to good effect. You soon begin to see progress occurring.

SEPTEMBER WEEK TWO

Neptune at opposition occurs at the end of this week. Neptune rules your house of dreams and healing. News is imminent, which features a blessing in disguise. It can feel like a paradox, a chapter ends, but this also creates a beginning which enables you to shift your focus forward. Releasing something outworn makes way for new experiences to come rushing in. It is a time of generating leads, seeking expansion and going after your dreams. An area you have been hoping to develop soon picks up momentum. You discover this venture does hold water. This encourages new ideas, your creative juices flow, you experience the ability to conceptualize a strategic path to obtain your vision. It does herald an exciting chapter, one which inspires and harnesses your trailblazing capabilities to good effect. A vibrant world of potential leaves you feeling inspired, you move out of your usual routine and connect with like-minded individuals. It does see you socializing and collaborating with others, it is a phase that expands your life, and this gets you involved with teamwork, discussions, and a pleasant social environment. An unexpected door opens, this brings an offer to your table that you find difficult to resist. Incredible changes occur, it heralds a time of developing your world in alignment with your heart. Personal growth is leading the charge forward, it does open a fresh cycle of options, which primarily relate to interpersonal bonds. Life is active, invitations arrived to tempt you out in a broader community environment. This forward motion is rejuvenating, it restores your spirit, and elevates your life. Life picks up speeds, and you kick off a chapter that helps you make great strides on your goals.

SEPTEMBER WEEK THREE

News arrives, which resets the potential surrounding you. It takes a moment to recalibrate and get with this new evolution. A bonus comes in your social life, exciting new possibilities create a stir when a dramatic entrance is made by a charismatic individual. It does guide you towards spontaneous adventures, you are in a phase of growth and expansion in your social life. New friendships are in the stars, a shift in perspective illuminates a path forward. A situation you nurture ripens in blossoms, drawing abundance into your life. A positive influence flows into your life, it brings enriching life experiences and underscores an atmosphere of change, harmony, and joy. You become more confident about moving out of your comfort zone and seeking out your tribe of kindred spirits. It does bring new options, and this sees you becoming involved in developing your life. You are less reactive and more proactive, engaging in energetic and creative thinking, you embrace the dynamic energy which arrives to stir up your life with new potential. Robust growth is coming; it draws a time of magic and manifestation. You have more control over the path ahead, and then you currently realize, or wielding your creative ideas, does bring stellar options into your life. Advancing your goals enables you to see a reward for the effort that you have contributed recently. It is a stirring chapter that is self-expressive, developmental, and productive. Fundamental changes are part of this episode, it does place a strong focus on doing the tasks necessary to get the rewards you seek.

SEPTEMBER WEEK FOUR

The Equinox this week arrives to allow you the ability to harness the power of manifestation. It illuminates a fantastic path where you can bring your goals together with a flourish. You launch into a phase that is big and bold; your potent creativity harnesses elements of manifestation to move you in a direction that is in alignment with your vision. You thrive on learning a new area; this brings growth as new ideas and projects cross your path, leaving you feeling inspired. Taking concrete actions towards achieving your goals does weave a fantastic basket of success. It is a vivid time which draws social expansion into your world. It does create forward-moving energy, being flexible, going with the flow, enables you to make the most of this dynamic phase. Lively conversations combine with fun banter, it is a blending of ideas and thoughts which set the stage for future progress. You feel energized by spending time with friends and family. Communication with your tribe is a vital aspect in the time ahead. A new friend is likely to make themselves known soon. Removing outworn energy, sees you grow in a new direction. Change is shifting you forwards, be mindful of signs, they help you forge a path towards an area which is in alignment with your higher purpose. A restless vibe is teaching you to reach for more. You discover you can create more potential by rearranging your life, creating space to draw something new into your life. You find that someone original, they have a quirky uniqueness that captures your attention. Sharing thoughts with this person could dramatically shift your focus forward. It culminates in a lively chapter, new goals and dreams are born under an azure sky.

OCTOBER ASTROLOGY

October 6 - New Moon in Libra.

The New Moon speaks of something new arriving in your world. This moon phase occurs at 11:05 UTC. This is an excellent time of the month to view galaxies and stars because there is no moonlight visible.

October 7 - Draconids Meteor Shower.

The Draconids meteor shower runs annually from October 6-10 and peaks this year on the night of the 7th.

October 8 – Mars in Conjunction with the Sun.

The planet Mars in Conjunction with the Sun. This occurs at 04:00 UTC.

October 9 – Mercury at Inferior Conjunction.

The planet Mercury at Inferior Conjunction. This planetary event occurs at 16:00 UTC.

October 13 – First Quarter Moon in Capricorn.

This Moon phase occurs at 03.25 UTC.

October 18 – Mercury Retrograde ends in Libra.

You can now move forward with any delayed plans that you have been putting off due to the Mercury Retrograde phase. Relationships should soon improve as miscommunications are overcome

October 20 - Full Moon in Aries.

The October full Moon is on the opposite side of the Earth as the Sun, and its face will be fully illuminated. This phase occurs at 14:57 UTC. This full moon is known as the Hunters Moon.

October 21, 22 - Orionids Meteor Shower.

The Orionids meteor shower runs yearly from October 2 to November 7. Orionids meteor shower peaks this year on the night of October 21 and the morning of October 22.

October 25 - Mercury at Greatest Western Elongation.

The planet Mercury reaches greatest western elongation of 18.4 degrees from the Sun. Look for Mercury low in the eastern sky just before sunrise. This event occurs at 05:00 UTC.

October 28 – Last Quarter Moon in Leo.

This Moon phase occurs at 20.05 UTC.

October 29 - Venus Greatest Eastern Elongation.

The planet Venus reaches its greatest eastern elongation of 47 degrees from the Sun. This is the best time to view Venus. Look for the bright planet Venus in the western sky after sunset. This planetary phase occurs at 22.00 UTC.

OCTOBER WEEK ONE

You are ready to connect with the broader world of potential, you discover an area that is worth developing soon. It brings a new zest to your life and does enable you to advance your situation. It's an essential time of personal growth, and indeed, it draws many gifts into your world. You won't be held back in the chapter ahead, things are ready to shift forward. This is a time that rules new options. Surprise information arrives, it enables you to gain insight into the past. While reflecting on your life's journey, you may be feeling sentimental about the passage of time. Taking time to release unresolved energy, does bring foundations which secure an essential shift forward. A pleasant surprise sees new potential flowing into your world. Soon, you plot a course towards an enterprising chapter. Pick your battles, focus on developing your goals, and seek a destination that is in alignment with your personality. Don't worry about what others have planned for your life, these are your dreams to chase, not theirs. A role is opening up for you soon. You have grown into someone with many gifts and talents. You have an exceptional ability to make the most of life, if you find that things are complicated, take time to balance your emotions, and be fully present as this draws clarity which will enable you to come up with the right solution. All in all, improvement in circumstances is an important theme ready to emerge for you.

OCTOBER WEEK TWO

Mars, in conjunction with the Sun this week, lets you pop the cork on the genie's bottle. This unleashes a beautiful bounty of new options. Surprise information draws an energizing chapter where you explore the possibilities and can plot a course towards developing new plans. You get the ball rolling on a new section, and as you unwrap the gifts ahead, you become more involved with nurturing your creativity. A trailblazing moment forward draws essential changes. It does have you thinking big about the possibilities, this is a transition phase. Currently, it can bring up memories for you to process. As you release the past, you connect with your vital force, which enables you to gain access to new ideas and possibilities. A refreshing change is coming; this beautiful alchemy brews an unusual path forward. Information is revealed that can be seen as a remarkable signpost. You have a tendency to give more than you receive. If there is anyone in your life who doesn't truly appreciate the efforts you bestow upon them, you would be correct if you limited contact. You are currently drawing activities that are suitable for your soul. It brings a journey that enables you to gain traction on improving your life and the quality of people you attract.

Information arrives, which inspires change. This puts you in the box seat to take advantage of a new path. You are ready to embrace a new chapter, you head to an area that catches your interest and are rewarded, quite unexpectedly, with a bonus. This brings favorable outcomes. A golden section is ready to blossom. Getting involved with developing your circumstances enables you more control over the path ahead than you currently realize.

OCTOBER WEEK THREE

This is a time which grows your world, it does bring a bounty which surprises and excites you. Constraints are lifted when Mercury Retrograde ends this week; your situation expands outwardly, enabling you to enjoy all that life has to offer. A sweet aspect of this time is that new potential is flowing into your world. It does bring good fortune and begins a path that has you meeting and making new friends. A cornucopia of opportunities is around the corner.

The Full Moon in Aries packs a stunning surprise, exciting news reaches you, it arrives suddenly, without warning, and it leaves you feeling blessed. You are the recipient of compelling information that draws a lucky break. This relates to something you have been watching and waiting for, as you see your situation improving, things line up most refreshingly. This spreads light over your world and observes something beautiful materializing in your life. This is a time which can be seen as unique, many of your dreams reach fruition. It does let you open a box of goodies, a plethora of new options are ready to blossom in your world. Don't worry about the past and the things that cannot be changed, right now, the future beckons, and it's as bright as Stardust.

A new option arrives, which helps you take advantage of a lucky break. This opportunity comes as a surprise, it brings great joy and sees you have an essential role on offer. You garner the attention of industry leaders, it does bring new friends and an enterprising course forward. It is a dazzling journey, rare and unique, this surprise rewards you for your dedication, concentration, and willingness to conquer challenges and reach for your goals.

OCTOBER WEEK FOUR

A new beginning is possible when a surprise crosses your path, your life symbolizes richness and fertility, this is an influence which draws abundance, you receive illuminating information which brings a trail that connects you to a meaningful journey. It does kick off a chapter which brings engaging and thoughtful conversations, you embark on developing goals and enjoy a more social environment. Information arrives, which balances your emotions and strengthens interpersonal bonds. It does see you drawing a chapter that holds the potential for growth and expansion. This incredible energy kicks off a phase that sets your mind ablaze with inspiration. It's a time of growing your world, the issues of the past soon fade into the backdrop of your life. It does bring a fantastic, energetic shift that faces you towards new goals. This is a time, which brings treasured memories into focus. You can appreciate the journey you have traveled, it does reflect your ability to navigate complexities and utilize the wisdom you have learned through the years. You diverge from your usual routine soon, and head off the beaten track, something arrives, which leads to a new trajectory, and exciting vision comes to life. A new option crosses your path, it does bring a memorable surprise. There is much on offer, looking at the road ahead, you see things coming together nicely. This gives you positive indications that you are on the right track to advance your world. You discover an area that is good for your soul, it is therapeutic, healing, and rejuvenating. Spending time developing your situation, you are rewarded with smooth sailing.

November 4 - New Moon in Scorpio.

The New Moon brings a clean chapter of potential. This phase occurs at 21:15 UTC. This is an excellent time to view the stars because there is no moonlight visible.

November 5 - Uranus at Opposition.

The blue-green planet will be at its closest approach to Earth, and its face will be fully illuminated by the Sun. This event occurs at 00:00 UTC.

November 11 – First Quarter Moon in Aquarius.

This Moon phase occurs at 12.46 UTC.

November 12 - Taurids Meteor Shower.

The Taurids meteor shower runs yearly from September 7 to December 10. It peaks on the night of November 12.

November 17 - Partial Lunar Eclipse

A partial lunar eclipse occurs when the Moon passes through the Earth's partial shadow or penumbra, only a portion of it passes through the umbra. During this eclipse, part of the Moon darkens as it moves through the Earth's shadow. This partial lunar eclipse will be visible throughout most of eastern Russia, Japan, the Pacific Ocean, North America, Mexico, Central America, and parts of western South America.

November 17, 18 - Leonids Meteor Shower.

The Leonids meteor shower runs yearly from November 6-30. The Leonids meteor shower peaks this year on the night of the 17th and morning of the 18th.

November 19 - Full Moon in Taurus.

The Full Moon is on the opposite side of the Earth as the Sun, and its face will be fully illuminated. This phase occurs at 08:58 UTC. This full moon is known as Full Beaver Moon.

November 27 – Last Quarter Moon in Virgo.

This Moon phase occurs at 12.28 UTC.

November 29 – Mercury at Superior Conjunction.

The planet Mercury at Superior Conjunction. This planetary event occurs at 05:00 UTC.

NOVEMBER WEEK ONE

The New Moon in Scorpio this week brings insight, clarity, and awareness. The energy of the past is coming up, this enables you to reflect on what has gone before, it can bring up sensitive emotions, this is part of the healing process, it improves the stability possible in your world by enabling you time to process difficult emotions, and resolve outworn energy. It is a time that helps you cut away from the deadwood and embrace a new flow of potential soon. It is a time where you make progress on a personal goal; this draws stability into your life, it brings you to a path which draws happiness and excitement into your world. As you embark on a new adventure, you stoke the fires of your inspiration, creativity is a crucial element which provides solutions. It does take you to an exciting chapter where you develop your life on your terms, it does see you connecting well others, there is a lot of activity coming to your social life, it does shine a light on deepening a bond which helps you progress your dreams. A new friendship arrives to stir the pot, and this adds the spice of excitement to your life. It does see you brew up a storm, and add a pinch of manifestation to the mix. Something you have been waiting for soon comes knocking, it does give you a positive indication that things are on the upswing. This leads to a more social time, which offers many blessings. It brings moments you treasure, it is your time to shine. A new chapter of life is coming, but fear not as evaluating your options, lets you move in alignment with your heart, and will draw abundance into your world.

NOVEMBER WEEK TWO

The Taurids meteor shower, which peaks on November 12th this year, see your potential shine brightly. It is a time of surprises and magic. An unexpected arrival brings joy into your world. A trip down memory lane with someone from the past is a wonderfully sentimental journey. This person holds you in high regard, they reconnect to make their feelings known. It may mark a big turning point for you, it brings a new option, you carry the wisdom of your past experiences with you. This person hopes to remain in touch with you moving forward. Surprise news arrives, which lights up your world. You start to reap the benefits from new energy, which brews a lucky break for you. It does expand your world, if you have found things restricted recently, this is set to change. It is a time which brings growth and expansion, your confidence is on the rise, fantastic news arrives to have you thinking about the possibilities. You see evidence of a new trend of abundance beginning to emerge. Your willingness to be open to change does see you staying on top of your game, you're in the box seat to progress your life, it is a time which supports growth as opportunities arrive that offer you a chance to develop your dreams. New potential opens the gateway, and an exciting option comes, this gives you something you can feel excited about exploring. You are ready to move forward, things are set to blossom in your world. Reviewing your progress does bring insight into your current trajectory. Taking all elements into consideration, you may decide to diverge off the current path and explore an area that is more in alignment with your creativity. It does see you finding the perfect outlet for self-expression, this is a smart move, it has you drawing abundance and new opportunities into your life. It is the perfect partnership for your future aspirations.

NOVEMBER WEEK THREE

A Partial Lunar Eclipse on the 17th brings healing. Things are going to be improving soon. It creates a shift forward, which amplifies your potential; you can leave issues behind you after this Lunar bath of rejuvenating energy. The Full Moon in Taurus occurs two days later and magnifies the effects of this lunar embrace. Working on your inner terrain this week is going to revolutionize your potential. It underscores a theme of change, healing, and evolution, which is flowing around your situation, guiding you to take more significant steps forward, do the work, which is necessary, and reap the results.

Additionally, you may be currently undervaluing your potential, a great deal can be achieved through expanding your horizons into virgin territory. Exploring new pathways to growth, lets you catch a lucky break soon when an area crops up which captures your interest. This is bringing new options into your life, you will have plenty to be grateful for, as it provides you with the wow factor. It is a lucky time with energy that revitalizes and leaves you feeling optimistic. This is drawing transformation and happiness into your life so that you can heal the past and embrace the future. You are given grace from above to expand your horizons out of your comfort zone. If there has been an area which has been testing your patience, things will resolve, it does see progress being made after a time of waiting for new information to arrive. You carve out time to focus your energy on areas that draw improvement. It does bring a chapter ruled by imagination and creativity; you discover results are possible using innovative solutions.

NOVEMBER WEEK FOUR

This week brims with new potential. You scope out an area which offers you room to harness a creative aspect. It is a time that brings hope, optimism, and surprising news. An offer reaches you which lands you in an environment of growth. You touched down in a landscape that offers room to grow your talents. You find this is the ideal time to reach for expansion and can accelerate your career trajectory. You are assertive in going after what you need, innovative and pioneering, it does see you making a move which advances your prospects. This is a time that is one of manifestation for you. It does bring you new options, home and family life blossoms, under sunny skies. New goals bring stable foundations, it does see you advancing your home situation, it offers you room to grow your life. A long-sought-after goal finally is achieved; this amplifies the abundance flowing into your life. It is a time that delivers good news, and that has you feeling on top of things. You go in strong and gain traction on achieving a robust phase of growth. It has you diving deep into new territory, you make significant progress, and hear good news, which is a result of the expansion you undertake. Putting your feelers out, you soon generate leads. News arrives, which is very exciting, you are ready to launch your ship into uncharted waters. It does ensure you create waves and make a splash.

December 4 - New Moon in Sagittarius.

The New Moon brings a clean slate of potential. This moon phase occurs at 07:43 UTC. This is an excellent time to view galaxies and stars because there is no moonlight visible.

December 4 – Total Solar Eclipse.

A total solar eclipse occurs when the moon completely blocks the Sun, revealing the Sun's outer atmosphere, which is called the corona. The path of totality will, for this eclipse, be limited to Antarctica and the southern Atlantic Ocean. A partial eclipse will bee visible throughout much of South Africa.

December 11 – First Quarter Moon in Pisces.

This Moon phase occurs at 01.36 UTC.

December 13, 14,15 - Geminids Meteor Shower.

The Geminids meteor shower runs each year from December 7-17. The Geminids meteor showers peaks this year on the night of the 13th, 14th, and 15th. The nearly new moon this year will provide dark skies for an excellent show. Best viewing will be from a dim vista after midnight. Meteors will radiate from the constellation Gemini but can appear anywhere in the sky.

December 19 - Full Moon in Gemini.

The Full Moon illuminates and draws clarity. This moon phase occurs at 04:36 UTC. This full moon is known as the Cold Moon and the Moon Before Yule.

December 21 - December Solstice.

The 2021 December solstice occurs at 15:59 UTC. The South Pole of the earth tilts toward the Sun, which, having reached its most southern place in the sky, is directly over the Tropic of Capricorn at 23.44 degrees south latitude. This December solstice also marks the first day of winter in the Northern Hemisphere.

December 21, 22 - Ursids Meteor Shower.

The Ursids meteor shower occurs each year from December 17 - 25. This meteor event peaks this year on the night of the 21st and morning of the 22nd.

December 27 – Last Quarter Moon in Libra.

This Moon phase occurs at 02.24 UTC.

DECEMBER WEEK ONE

December hits the right kind of positive note that you need in your life. It brings an exciting opportunity to expand your consciousness. If life has felt limited or shrouded recently, you soon lift the lid on a new chapter. Creativity and imagination light up new ideas; you launch a project which is a winning endeavor. It does bring an environment that spotlights community involvement, you fill your life with supportive and treasured friends. A situation you nurture blossoms into a profound bond. You certainly open a new chapter and trigger beautiful possibilities, it lights a path of friendship and fun. You have more options to socialize, it is a sparkling journey which enables you to increase your circle of friends and acquaintances. You develop new pathways of growth. It rules expansion that draws excitement. Hopes and wishes are no longer on hold, you see progress being made, a long-held dream suddenly reaches fruition. It is an enchanting time which draws magic into your life. It is the new beginning you have been seeking. You encounter attractive new options that reveal magic and abundance flowing into your life. There is a strong emphasis on heightened social activity, it shifts your focus forward, and this has you connecting with new friends. It is a time of expanding options, you enter a prestigious environment, it does grow your career path. Mixing with influencers, you obtain a proposal that provides a way that advances your situation. Achieving your goals brings recognition, a burst of energy arrives to shift your focus forward.

DECEMBER WEEK TWO

A dramatic surprise arrives, which helps you create change, it opens a new chapter, and it is a powerful boost that allows you to plot a course towards success. This astonishing information greets you with a blessing you can expand upon. Something comes up out of the blue, taking full advantage of this possibility, draws luck and good fortune into your life. It makes this season bigger and brighter for you. Something refreshing is ready to zing into your life. It does lift your spirits, it's a superb time to plot a course towards achieving your dreams. The path ahead is paved with glittering options, it helps shift your focus forward with a new and exciting venture. This Christmas is all about the bling. A wonderful present is ready to be revealed, it does leave you feeling breathless, a meaningful moment glitters with a golden sentiment. It does see a situation moving forward, and this lights a delightful path ahead. You receive a beautiful gift from someone who cares about you. Something you have been hoping for reaches a culmination, enabling new goals to emerge. This is a time that is ripe with new projects and dreams to inspire your mind. It does kick off a prosperous phase where you plot a course towards future goals. It is a great time to manifest a long-held dream, and having a smart strategy in place, lets you avoid common pitfalls that could derail progress. A window is opening, harmony is ready to breeze into your life. This is a time which brings a great chance to integrate various elements of your life, you absorb and resolve emotions which have complicated your life. Soul-searching brings a few epiphanies about areas that need work, and where to shift your focus next. Releasing the past opens the door on a lighter and brighter future. It's has you emerging from this chaotic chapter, ready to embrace a new flow of potential.

DECEMBER WEEK THREE

If your energy has been feeling depleted recently, you are set to experience a lift that helps stabilize and restore your foundations. A new flow of inspiration generates an exciting chapter, it gives you a burst of motivation to accomplish a long thought of goal. It is a particular time where you have more to look forward to, as it also brings the news out of the blue to inspire a phase of growth. This is an ideal time to refresh your vision, there is new inspiration arriving soon, if you currently feel at a crossroads, understanding the direction ahead does enable you to gain progress on an exciting journey forward. There is more time to focus on your creativity next year; it does draw self-development and nurtures your talents. You make headway on your goals by plotting a possible and logical trajectory. It does bring a fascinating chapter that offers remarkable changes. You begin a path that provides a room to grow your talents. It does light up your life favorably, and there is an area that emerges that is highly beneficial to you. Many new options are arriving, expect exciting news to bring gifts and luck into your world. You undertake an essential course or learning endeavor, it paves the way for your passion to be ignited. The journey ahead is littered with golden opportunities, moving in alignment with your vision, you are lifted towards your goals. While it is a lofty goal, you are more than capable of achieving this daring vision. It does bring recognition, it gives you the support needed to fund your journey, you discover this is something worth exploring. It's a lovely time spent focused around home and family this week. Little goes under the radar as you spot an opportunity that feels like the right fit for your situation. It does enable you to create more substantial changes around your lofty goals.

DECEMBER WEEK FOUR

This has been a big month for you. It takes you to a time where there is a fork in the road. This is a quiet time that allows you to think about future goals and plot a course for all that you hope to accomplish. It is a creative time that draws blessings into your life. It helps filter out distractions and places a spotlight on getting to the heart of what your vision is going to be. You can harness an aspect of manifestation to bring your dreams to life. You have an open road to new possibilities ready to be explored. It does bring a focus on improving your situation. It draws happy news which enables you to feel that things are coming together. A shimmering path emerges which delivers the perfect atmosphere to develop a personal goal. A secret is revealed which gives you insight into the past; it draws healing and lets you make peace with what has gone before. It's a great time that sees personal development occurring. It seems you grow your vision as bright news arrives to give you a boost. It shines a light on a powerful chapter which brings new opportunities and helps you extend your influence outwardly, you ratchet up the possibilities for creative thinking, and explore a path which is different to your regular routine, contributing your ideas to your broader audience draws new friendships. It does give you an excellent chance to advance your vision, you hit your stride and illuminate glittering new options. This is a particularly unique time for you; it does see more social opportunities arrive which nurtures your soul. It is the perfect recipe for renewal, rejuvenation, and kicking back with your kindred spirits. An invitation to an event arrives and this is extra special, you mark this in your calendar, and look forward to an exciting and vibrant time. There is plenty to be inspired about over the coming weeks, it is a time of abundance.

Dear Stargazer,

I hope you have enjoyed planning your year with the stars utilizing Astrology and Zodiac influences. My zodiac star sign books are released each year, which detail a monthly list of astrological events, and a weekly (four weeks to a month) horoscope. You can find me on my Facebook page where you can get personal astrology or intuitive readings.

https://www.facebook.com/SiaSands

Instagram: SiaSands

See my full list of books here:

https://www.SiaSands.com

Leaving a review is welcomed and appreciated.

Many Blessings,

Sia Sands